A Splash of Welcome Water

by Elizabeth Thiel Engfer

This book is presented to

_____

by

_____

_____

date

Augsburg Fortress, Minneapolis

Splashy, flashy—water
from clouds and rivers,
Trickily, ripply—water
in puddles and ponds,
Drippy, droppy—water
from faucets and hydrants,
Rushy, crushy—water
in oceans and falls.

Cool water, wet water,
Fresh-me water,
new-me water!
A splash of welcome water
is God's gift of love.

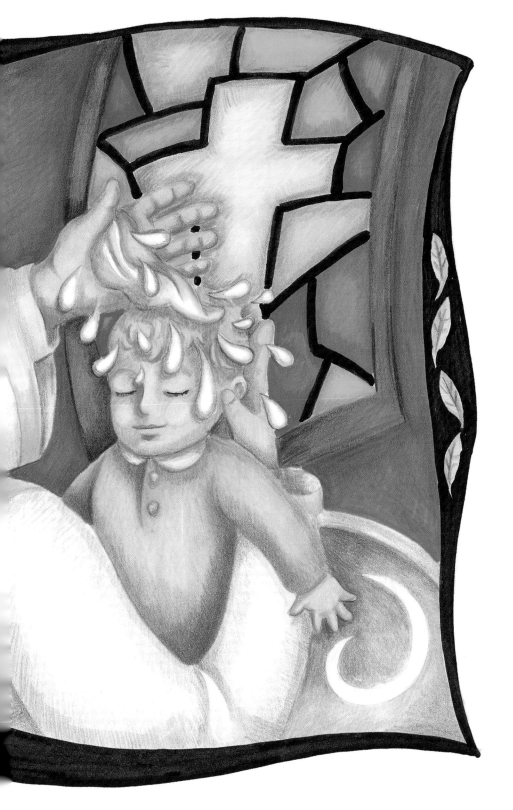

Splash! Little Zoe plays in the ocean. In the United States, where she lives, it can be hot and dry in summer. Cool water feels good on a sunny day.

Zoe's parents bring her to church. It is her baptism day. **Splash!** The pastor pours water on her head, then makes the sign of the cross. Zoe feels the cool water and wiggles. The people in church smile. "We welcome you into God's family!" they say.

Splash! It's raining in Namibia where Olivia and Charles live. Drip, drip goes the rain into a barrel. Olivia and Charles take a bath in the warm rainwater. They want to be clean for church.

Going into church with
Mama, Olivia and Charles
pass the baptismal font.
"Today is your special
day," whispers Mama.
"God loves us!
Good news!" sing the
choir and congregation.
When Olivia and Charles
bend down at the font,
the pastor scoops lots of
water on their heads.
Splash! "In Baptism,
God washes away your
sins," he says. "By God's
grace you are clean
and new!"

Splash! Thirsty Marco gets a drink from the pump. Then he fills a pitcher for his family—Papa, Mama, Grandmother, and baby Cristina. "Agua. Water," says Grandmother, smiling. "Gracias. Thanks, Marco. I think our water is the best in all of Mexico."

Marco's family is joining Grandmother's church. Papa, Mama, Marco, and Cristina are baptized together. "In the name of the Father, the Son, and the Holy Spirit," says the pastor as he drenches them with water.
Splash! "God promises to be with you always." The pastor gives Marco a candle to light every year to remember his family's baptism day.

Splash! Chiu Fong soaks his
little garden on the roof with water.
He is growing vegetables in big pots.
In Hong Kong most people don't have yards.
Chiu Fong will share the food with friends at church.

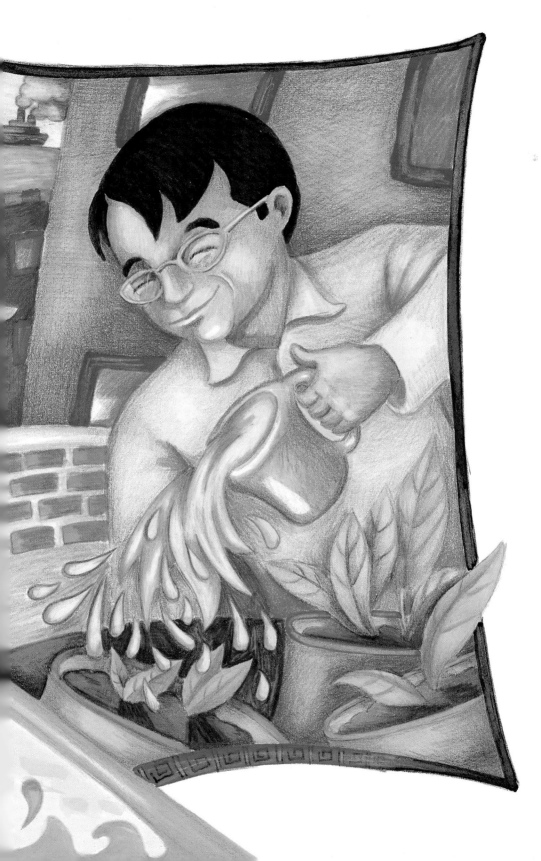

A friend gave Chiu Fong a Bible and invited him to church. Chiu Fong is so happy to learn about God's love that he wants to be baptized. "Baptism is a gift from God," the pastor tells him as he comes up and out of the water. Splash! "God's Spirit will help you grow. Peace be with you!"

The welcome water
of Baptism reminds us of God's
promises to us. God loves us and
welcomes us into the church family.
God forgives us when we do
wrong things. God is always with us,
helping us grow.

Splash! God's welcome water touches you too. You are God's child! God loves you—now and forever.